CONTENTS

Looking at Privilege and Power

Kelly Glass

Publishing
treet
Y 10011
slow.com

Published in 2019 by Enslow Publishing, LLC.
101 W. 23rd Street, Suite 240, New York, NY 10011

Library of Congress Cataloging-in-Publication Data

Names: Glass, Kelly, author.
Title: Looking at privilege and power / Kelly Glass.
Description: New York : Enslow Publishing, [2019] | Series: Racial literacy | Audience:
    Grade 7–12. | Includes bibliographical references and index.
Identifiers: LCCN 2018019106| ISBN 9781978504677 (library bound) | ISBN
    9781978505629 (pbk.)
Subjects: LCSH: Privilege (Social psychology) | Power (Social sciences) | Social justice.
Classification: LCC HM671 .G545 2019 | DDC 303.3/72—dc23
LC record available at https://lccn.loc.gov/2018019106

Printed in the United States of America

To Our Readers: We have done our best to make sure all website addresses in this book were active and appropriate when we went to press. However, the author and the publisher have no control over and assume no liability for the material available on those websites or on any websites they may link to. Any comments or suggestions can be sent by email to customerservice@enslow.com.

Introduction

On February 14, 2018, a nineteen-year-old shooter walked into affluent Marjory Stoneman Douglas High School in Parkland, Florida, and opened fire, killing seventeen people and wounding as many. It was one of the world's most tragic and deadliest school shootings. Of the many things known about the shooter, it was reported that he talked about hating Black people, Mexicans, and gay people. On March 7, 2018, the shooter was indicted on seventeen counts of first-degree murder and seventeen counts of attempted first-degree murder.

The school reopened a couple of weeks later, and safety measures were instituted. Instead of the usual initial grief and brief discussion about solutions to this country's mass shooting problem, some of the survivors of this historical tragedy made sure this played out a little differently than the shootings before. Emma Gonzalez, Jaclyn Corin, and David Hogg started the #NeverAgain movement—challenging lawmakers to end these mass school murders. They went straight to those in power.

Marjory Stoneman Douglas High School students share the stage with other gun violence survivors at the March for Our Lives rally in Washington, DC, on March 24, 2018.

At the March for Our Lives Rally, Hogg called out the media for not giving the Black students a voice. Corin made an even stronger statement when she said, "We recognize that Parkland received more attention because of its affluence, but we share this stage today and forever with those communities who have always stared down the barrel of a gun."[1]

Corin shared her stage, literally and figuratively. She brought Yolanda Renee King, Martin Luther King Jr.'s granddaughter, to the stage. They also brought Naomi Wadler, a Black student from Virginia, to speak on behalf of all the "African-American girls whose stories don't make the front page of every national newspaper."[2] The conversation spread to a March for Our Lives rally all the way in Chicago, a city plagued with gun violence long before the mass shooting on Valentine's Day 2018 in Parkland, Florida. Most Chicago public school students have never felt safe at their schools. The students of Marjory Stoneman Douglas High School in Parkland, Florida, recognized it was the positioning of their school as a predominantly white high school in an affluent area that gave them a platform, and they used that platform to invite people of color to the table. When privilege is used correctly, it is a tool that works to bring diversity, inclusivity, and equality. When used incorrectly, it is a weapon that oppresses. Like any good tool, we must first learn about it— what it is, how it works, and what to do with it.

CHAPTER 1

Privilege and Power Explained

Each student in a classroom is given a piece of paper to crumple up. The trash can is positioned in the front of the room, and the teacher explains the game. The class makes up the population of America, and each student has a chance to "move up" in life by simply tossing the balled-up paper in the bin. The students in the back rows of the class complain about the obvious unfair advantage of their peers near the front of the class, but the students in those front rows just see the wealth and opportunity that's within reach. This anecdotal explanation of privilege gets a lot right about power and privilege.

Those who benefit from privilege are largely unaware or rarely want to admit it. Like the students in the front of the class in the example above, they only see their own starting line and the seemingly attainable goals in front of them. With that perspective, the obstacles in the way of those in the rows behind them seem imaginary. *I had to work hard to make that basket. No one helped me. They just need to work harder.*

A simple exercise using a waste basket and balled up sheets of paper is a good starting point to begin the conversation about privilege in a classroom setting.

The positioning of the students in the classroom gave some of them an unfair advantage. In this scenario, the students had done nothing in particular to earn a spot at the front of the class. The students in the back of the class hadn't necessarily done anything to deserve being in the back. All students, however, were presented with what seemed to be the same opportunity. In real-world examples of privilege, the obstacles are not placed by one individual person but rather a result of a set of systems put in place to maintain the power the dominant group has established. In America, that dominant group is whites, hence the term "white privilege."

Privilege Defined

The sociological definition of privilege is unearned advantages and power given to some people because they belong to a certain group. White privilege in particular refers to the resources, access, and power systematically given to white people at the expense of people of color. The term itself can be traced back to 1935, when Black American sociologist and civil rights activist W. E. B. Du Bois wrote about the "white skin privilege" in his book *Black Reconstruction in America.*[1] Du Bois described how whiteness serves as a "public and psychological wage" that gives power and privilege to even lower-class white laborers:[2]

> "They were admitted freely with all classes of white people to public functions, public parks, and the best schools. The police were drawn from their ranks, and the courts, dependent on their votes, treated them with such leniency as to encourage lawlessness. Their vote selected public officials, and while this had small effect upon the economic situation, it had great effect upon their personal treatment and the deference shown them. White schoolhouses were the best in the community, and conspicuously placed, and they cost anywhere from twice to ten times as much per capita as the colored schools."[3]

Even though the Great Depression of 1929–1939 gravely impacted all Americans, Black Americans were hit the hardest, as poor white workers benefited from white privilege. The unemployment rate for Black workers was two to three times more than that of whites.[4] White workers called for Blacks to be fired and those jobs given to whites.

Street scene from Harlem in 1935, which was hit much harder than the rest of New York City by the Great Depression.

What the Term "People of Color" (POC) Really Means

Historically, the terms "colored people" and "persons of color" were reserved for those of African ancestry. Today, it covers people of African, Native American, Asian or Pacific Islander, and Latinx/Hispanic ancestry. The term "people of color" is meant to be inclusive, but it's important to note that it is really meant to emphasize the common experience of marginalized racial and ethnic groups.

Power and Oppression

White workers during the Great Depression exercised their white privilege because whites had, and continue to have, access to most of the power in our society. Privilege is a result of power structures that were established by the dominant group. In America, a country founded upon the genocide of Native Americans and built upon the enslavement of Africans by white people, the oppression of groups of people has historically served as a means to keep whites in power.

Slavery by Many Other Names

Throughout the seventeenth century, white settlers stole African people from their homes, tearing apart families, to bring cheap and plentiful labor to the New World. This forced labor stripped the enslaved Africans of their legal and most basic rights under the guise of white supremacy. The same US Constitution that called for "equality, liberty, and justice for all" defined the often beaten and tortured slaves as three-fifths of a person. Whites rationalized the inhumane treatment of slaves by considering them property, not human beings. When slavery was abolished in 1865, the effects of this race-based system of white control lingered. The Black Codes—state laws design to restrict the freedom of newly freed slaves—required Blacks to sign labor contracts or be arrested and forced into unpaid labor.[5] Once these

George Washington talks to an overseer on his farm in Mount Vernon, Virginia, as several slaves harvest hay.

laws were overturned and the 14th and 15th Amendments provided Blacks due process and the right to vote, whites feared the political and economic power that Blacks stood to gain. Jim Crow laws were born. Jim Crow laws segregated schools, restaurants, and reinforced the idea that Blacks were inferior, and as such, kept them in inferior conditions and systematically denied basic rights and services. Fast-forward to today, when both slavery and Jim Crow laws have been legally overturned. The same systems and beliefs that kept those policies working now send a disproportionate number of Black people to prison, where cheap labor is again the name of the game.

Privilege and oppression are two sides of the same coin, with whites staying in power the main goal. When combined with prejudice, power is a key component to racism. Even without the presence of prejudice, however, exercising power and privilege results in the oppression of those not in power. Because America has historically used race and racist ideals as an excuse to cruelly and unjustly keep other groups restrained and under authority, racial oppression was essentially woven into the very fabrics of our institutions.[6]

CHAPTER 2

Examining White Privilege

Whiteness is the default in American society, and that has consequences for people of color. The oppression of people of color in America serves to benefit white people. Whether actively or passively, white Americans benefit from white privilege—that is, the advantages of being white, and not a person of color, in a society where whites hold the power and the country's institutions were designed to keep it that way. Of course, admitting to benefitting from racism and the oppression of other people is not easy. It's especially a challenge because many of the people who do benefit don't even realize how.

The Invisibility of White Privilege

According to a Pew Research Center survey, 58 percent of Americans say racism is a "big problem in our society," while 29 percent say it is "somewhat of a problem."[1] This suggests that racism is widely acknowledged as an existing problem, so why is it hard to see the other side?

Scholar and anti-racism activist Peggy McIntosh, who is credited with bringing the term "white privilege" to the mainstream, calls white privilege an invisible knapsack of tools and resources that white people possess but were meant to be oblivious to. McIntosh says, "As a white person, I realized I had been taught about racism as something which puts others at a disadvantage, but had been taught not to see one of its corollary aspects, white privilege, which puts me at an advantage."[2]

With these benefits and advantages available to them, white people do and will come across social and economic hardships. White privilege is not an immunity to trials and obstacles. When those hardships do occur, however, white people have tools or advantages at their disposal in their

A chalk drawing in Union Square Park in New York City depicts the names of Black men, women, and children shot and killed by police.

invisible knapsacks that people of color do not. Those invisible knapsacks also hold keys with access to our country's social institutions.

White Privilege in Education

After the Civil War and the freeing of the slaves, who were not allowed to read or write, freed Blacks sought education in informal ways. They were not allowed in white schools. *Brown v. Board of Education* was the Supreme Court case that finally outlawed school segregation in 1954. Desegregation took several more years, and consequently, Black American students do not start on the same playing field as white students.

According to US Department of Education data from 2012, Black students are six times more likely to attend high-poverty schools than white students.[3] High-poverty schools are schools where more than 75 percent of students meet the income guidelines for free and reduced lunch, tend to have overfilled classrooms, lack highly qualified and experienced teachers, college prerequisite courses, textbooks and technology, and extracurricular activities.[4] The majority of white students, on the other hand, go to schools where they have the opportunity to take courses that prepare them for college, fill their résumés with extracurricular activities, and have access to the textbooks and technology required for their coursework.[5] School districts assign the least experienced teachers to high-minority, high-poverty schools.[6] One study of 500 school districts found that, with no respect to income level, the more Black students at a school, the

Nettie Hunt sits on the steps of the US Supreme Court with her three-year-old daughter on May 18, 1954, the day after the court ruled that segregation in public schools is unconstitutional.

less funding that school received.[7] Historical educational inequities have kept Black students from receiving even the same quality education as their white peers. Though segregation was legally outlawed, white students still benefit from its legacy and are overall receiving more attention in smaller classrooms, more resources, and access to more experienced teachers and better educations—all by virtue of being born white.

Linda Brown of *Brown v. Board of Education*

Linda Brown was nine years old when her father tried to enroll her at the elementary school closest to their home in Topeka, Kansas. The all-white elementary school was just a few blocks away, but Brown had to bus miles across town to attend school with the other Black children. Her father filed a lawsuit against the Board of Education, claiming that segregation in public schools was unconstitutional. In May 1954, the Supreme Court ruled that "separate educational facilities are inherently unequal" and a violation of the 14th Amendment.[8] It took years to desegregate schools—and many have resegregated over time as the courts have failed to enforce desegregation plans—but the landmark ruling helped dismantle segregation in all public facilities. Brown died on March 25, 2018, but her legacy lives.

The children at the center of **Brown v. Board of Education,** *from front,* **Vicki Henderson, Donald Henderson, Linda Brown, James Emanuel, Nancy Todd,** *and* **Katherine Carper.**

Understanding Whiteness and White-Passing Privilege

The US Census Bureau defines "white" as a person whose origins are any of the original peoples of Europe, the Middle East, or North Africa. The Census Bureau also explains that the purpose of such racial categories is to reflect the social definition of race recognized in this country and is not an attempt to define race biologically.[9] Yes—race is a social construct. Social constructs were created by society, namely the majority, for a reason. Whiteness in America was created as the norm against which all other groups are to be compared. In this context, appearing to be white even when biologically a person of color can often afford some privileges. This white-passing privilege is complicated because it is so conditional, which means it depends on the situation. White-passing people, for example, may benefit from whiteness systemically while individually still be exposed to the negative stereotypes of the groups they identify with. Because of this experience, it's important to recognize white-passing privilege but also recognize that it is not the same experience as white privilege.

Economic White Privilege

Once in the job market, whites continue to benefit even more. The unemployment rate for white people is typically half of what it is for Black people and lower than that of Hispanics.[10] Even among the college educated the disparity exists. The unemployment rate on average for college-educated Blacks, in particular, is 34 percent higher than that of Hispanics and 93 percent higher than that of whites with the same level of college education.[11] White privilege does not mean white people do not face unemployment. It means they experience it at far fewer rates than people of color—even in crisis. During economic recessions, whites still face far less unemployment than Blacks and Hispanics.

The job search is also more advantageous for white job seekers. In one study, researchers responded to help wanted ads in newspapers with fake résumés. The résumés differed in one way—some of the fake applicants had commonly white-associated names while the others had stereotypically Black names. The applications with the "white" names received 50 percent more job interviews.[12] Though two candidates may have similar experience, credentials, and education, white

White privilege is evident in the workplace, from the hiring process to the income gap and opportunities for advancement.

privilege gives the white candidate the upper hand in landing the job. When a job offer is not extended, the white candidate doesn't have to wonder if it was race-based discrimination that caused them to be denied employment. More than likely, the people hiring were white, too.

The Income Gap

The benefits of being white extend beyond the search process. Large racial and gender wage gaps in the United States remain, even as they have narrowed in some cases over the years. Whites earn about one dollar to every 75 cents a Black person makes.[13] Among those with college degrees, the income gap still persists. College-educated Black and Hispanic men make about 80 percent less than white college-educated men. College-degree-holding Black and Hispanic women earn only about 70 percent of what white men make.[14] A white person with the same education and experience as a person of color will earn significantly more money over a lifetime. As such, whites continue to build a generational economic advantage over people of color. In 2011, the median value of wealth and assets for a white household was $132,483, compared to $9,211 for the median Black household.[15] Because wealth is transferred between generations, the racial income gap and the wealth gap help perpetuate and support economic white privilege and, consequently, economic injustice.

White Privilege and Media Representation

The media—film, television, print news, and all the ways we receive mass communication—helps shape and uphold our ideas about race and ethnicity. It plays an important role in shaping the way we understand society and the world around us. The representations of groups of people that we see affect us. American television and film also play an important role in upholding white privilege. In recent years, #OscarsSoWhite attempted to call out the overrepresentation of white people and the invisibility of Blacks, Hispanics, and Asians in film. Research suggests that not seeing people of the same race, or other identifying factors, in film and television means that you are somehow unimportant.[16] Also, when people of color are represented in the media, the representations are overwhelmingly negative. For example, one study determined that Blacks were overrepresented as criminals in news and opinion media while only 28 percent of criminal representations were white, compared to the actual 77 percent of whites arrested for criminal activity.[17] Media representations in television and film humanize white people while demonizing people of color.

White privilege is most notably evident in news coverage of crime. On June 17, 2016, Dylann Roof walked into a prayer service at Emanuel African Methodist Episcopal Church

Actors J. K. Simmons, Patricia Arquette, Julianne Moore, and Eddie Redmayne pose with their Oscars for best actor and best actress awards at the 87th Annual Academy Awards.

in Charleston, South Carolina. He was welcomed into the church, and with him he carried a gun he bought with birthday money despite a previous drug possession charge that should have barred him from purchasing it. He opened fire, coldly and methodically killing nine Black people. After a manhunt, Roof was pulled over and arrested, and the arresting officers bought him a burger because he was hungry.[18]

The events leading up to the crime and the crime itself are a grand example of white privilege at work, and the news coverage of the crime continued the narrative. Major media outlets were reluctant to call it terrorism, a descriptor freely given to non-white mass shooters. Instead of headlines digging into his criminal past, as in the case of Black police-shooting victims Michael Brown, Philando Castile, and many others, headlines laid out sympathy for his "trouble at home and school" and his "father's bitter divorce."[19] In grave contrast to the criminalization of Black police-shooting victims after their deaths, Dylann Roof and other white gunmen are consistently humanized by the media.

CHAPTER 3

Intersections of Privilege and Oppression

Privilege does not occur in a vacuum. It manifests in the ways other groups of people are oppressed. It benefits the dominant group at the expense of minority groups. Privilege certainly doesn't function as a monolith for any group, but to understand privilege and how it functions, it is necessary to understand the groups of people on the other side of it. Feminist theorist Marilyn Frye describes oppression as a specially designed cage:

> "The experience of oppressed people is that the living of one's life is confined and shaped by forces and barriers which are not accidental or occasional and hence avoidable, but are systematically related to each other in such a way as to catch one between and among them and restrict or penalize motion in any direction. It is the experience of being caged in: all avenues, in every direction, are blocked or booby trapped."[1]

Who Is Oppressed?

White people in America hold power over people of color by maintaining control over the country's institutions, laws, rules, and societal norms. People of color are as a result mistreated, subject to discrimination, and not privy to the same advantages as white people.[2] People of color in this country are oppressed through racism. Other groups of people are also systematically oppressed.

Women

Women have been denied equal rights throughout American history. Historically, many laws and policies have worked to systematically oppress women by denying them the right to own property, work certain jobs, inherit wealth, and make decisions regarding their own bodies. For decades, women petitioned for the right to vote. The Constitution was finally ratified in 1920, and that year more than eight million women voted for the first time.[3] History, dating as far back as biblical times, placed men in dominant roles, and men's desire to keep that power and control contributes to the oppression of women. Though women today are *legally* granted rights, male privilege still permeates in America's patriarchal society. Economically, women make about 77.9 cents for every one dollar that men make.[4] Women are 85 percent less likely to hold executive positions in companies and organizations.[5]

Class photo of the 113th Congress on the steps of the US Capitol

Women are also underrepresented in government—women make up about 51 percent of the US population yet only 20 percent of Congress. Male privilege has contributed to rape culture, where one out of every five women has been raped.[6] The sexist microaggressions—the everyday abuses and hostile, derogatory actions toward marginalized people—that men perpetrate against women are so common that they have gone largely under the radar until recent social media movements such as #MeToo and #YesAllWomen where women have shared stories of violence against them.[7]

The Poor

About four million people live in poverty in America. The poor are often discussed as a group of lazy people who just need to work harder. In reality, poverty is a result of economic oppression, economic exploitation, and a social system that relies on keeping certain people poor. Typically performing hard or undesired labor for minimum wage, the poor remain stuck in a cycle fueled by the business and economic needs of the wealthy for low-cost labor. When adjusted for inflation, or the increase in prices and fall in the purchasing value of money, the minimum wage peaked in 1968, when the average cost of a house was about $15,000.[8,9] With home values outpacing inflation, it is nearly impossible for the working poor to own property, build generational wealth, and break out of the poverty cycle.

LGBTQ+

Lesbian, gay, bisexual, transgender, queer, and intersex people face oppression, rejection, discrimination, harassment, and

Contrary to popular belief, the poor in this country are usually hardworking people stuck in a cycle of poverty with little opportunity for career advancement.

violence. LGBTQ+ youth are 120 percent more likely to experience homelessness, according to a youth homelessness study.[10] They are often forced out of their homes due to lack of acceptance. This is compounded by hiring discrimination, which makes it more difficult for LGBTQ+ people to find

Although all people living below the poverty line are at risk of homelessness, LGBTQ+ youth are more likely to become homeless after being kicked out of their parents' homes.

jobs compared to straight, cisgendered people. They are also more likely to experience a hate crime than any other marginalized group. LGBTQ+ people are still fighting for many rights and recognitions. In thirty-one states, there are no explicit anti-discrimination employment protections for transgender people.

The Disabled

Mentally and physically disabled people navigate a society where their differences are perceived as weaknesses. The iden-tity of the able-bodied is considered normal and preferred. The power given to able-bodied people works to make the obstacles faced by disabled people more and more invisible. Public buildings, homes, transportation, social gatherings, education, and the workplace are all designed for the able-bodied. Disabled people are chronically underemployed and more

Disabled people face daily reminders that the world they live in was not designed with them in mind. Even existing in and navigating public spaces can be an obstacle.

likely to live in poverty than people without disabilities.[11] Children with disabilities are almost four times more likely to experience violence than children without disabilities.[12] The Americans with Disabilities Act, which also includes people

with mental illness and substance addiction, prohibits discrimination against people with disabilities, but intentional disregard as well as ignorance of the law still occur.

How These Identities Intersect

The oppressed social groups listed above are not fully comprehensive. Religious minorities such as Muslims, immigrants of color, and the elderly are also oppressed in some ways. The most important takeaway is there is privilege in being white, hetereosexual, upper class, Christian, cisgender, able-bodied, and male. White privilege doesn't function the same for every white person, but it does function—even when it intersects with other identities.

To a poor white person, the phrase "white privilege" feels like a slap in the face. The story becomes about the poor white people who came from nothing and worked their way up with no regard to how they were allowed to move so freely upward. Education is often touted as the key, but people of color have to face an educational system that has lower expectations and fewer resources for them. What about hard work? If people of color are unemployed, they must not be trying, right? White people don't have to worry about being discriminated against because of negative stereotypes about their work ethic or English being a second language, even if they are recent immigrants. White privilege also allows white people to buy homes and start businesses without facing the loan discrimination that people of color face at banks. At every turn, people of color face obstacles that white people enjoying the American Dream take for granted.

Another important example of this intersectionality is white women and white privilege. The Women's March of 2017 brought women from across the country to Washington, DC, to advocate for women's rights. The large group of mostly white women donned pink hats to symbolize their vaginas. This sentiment of the pink hats failed to take into account people of color as well as transgender and nonbinary people without typical female genitalia. The voices of white women were centered at the expense of women of color, whose women's rights issues include the effects of mass incarceration on their communities, lack of access to quality and affordable health care, threat of deportation, and violence and murder committed against trans women. Even the event itself, protesting in large, hard-to-maneuver crowds, excluded disabled people.

In the same way oppressed and privileged identities can intersect, so can more than one oppressed identity. LGBTQ+ young people of color are more likely to experience homelessness than their white peers.[13] They are also twice as likely to experience hiring discrimination than white LGBTQ+ youth.[14] People with intersectional marginalized identities are more vulnerable to various types of discriminations working together to do the oppressing. It's also important to note that poverty is not only a cause but a consequence

Women protest for women's rights at the Women's March on January 21, 1016.

of the oppression of marginalized groups and is one area where people of color, disabled, and LGBTQ+ people are disproportionately represented compared to white people. So while white people can and will have oppressed identities intersecting with their whiteness, they are still presented with the advantages and benefits of being white.

CHAPTER 4

The Myths of Privilege

Privilege is a social reality. Like other social realities, it's often stereotyped and oversimplified, leading to myths and misunderstandings of the concept. White privilege does not necessarily look like a white man from an upper-middle-class family who attends a private high school, goes on to an Ivy League institution, and gets a high-paying job with a corner office and a huge house in the suburbs. White privilege can be seen in the way white children freely play with toy guns and play fight, while Black children are taught to avoid such behavior that could be mistaken as real and potentially cost them their lives. It's seen in the way people of color search for books and movies with people that look like them while white people, who have no shortage of representation in the media, question why "color" matters. It's how white people can go shopping without the anxiety of what to do with their hands to ensure people know they aren't stealing.

White children are able to play with toy guns—a luxury that Black children cannot afford without the risk of being shot, arrested, or otherwise deemed a threat.

Even everyday language exemplifies white privilege. The word "ghetto" is often used to describe things associated with Black people. It reinforces the idea that Black, and everything associated with Blackness, is undesirable. Expressing to a Mexican American surprise at how they speak "good English" is another example of a subtle expression of white privilege. These microaggressions—the everyday intentional and unintentional negative, hostile messages communicated to marginalized people—have a cumulative adverse effect on the receivers. These messages communicate to people of color that they are lesser, inferior, and do not belong. They affect the receivers negatively on a personal level, but they also work on a larger level to reinforce power structures and white privilege. Understanding these and other nuances of white privilege at work can help unpack the myths and stereotypes surrounding this important concept.

"Poor White People Don't Have Privilege"

White privilege is real—even for poor white people. One of the main determinants of quality of life is location, and poor white people are less likely to live in concentrated areas of poverty than poor Black people. A poor Black family is much more likely than a poor white family to live in a neighborhood with other poor families.[1] This double burden of poverty means that while white families are allowed to spread out in most metropolitan cities, Black families are segregated and left with the burden of not only their own poverty but the disadvantages that come with being in a poor neighborhood (high-poverty schools, and lack of access to fresh foods and other resources, for example).

"It's About Class, not Race"

Because white people are much less likely than Black people to live in concentrated areas of poverty, they are not subject to the same heightened presence of police using aggressive tactics for even minor infractions, also known as over-policing. A major consequence of living in concentrated areas of poverty is the vicious cycle of biased targeting and suspicion of people of color and the subsequent high incarceration rates that cause poor families of color to lose income earners, sending them even deeper into poverty. This phenomenon of biased targeting and suspicion of POC, known as racial profiling, is certainly symptomatic of white privilege. Research shows that police mainly protect the interests of white and affluent people.[2] Because of that, and because poverty is seen as a threat to those with such privileges, city governments are likely to increase police force strength in high-poverty areas.[3] One example of this is known as driving while Black (or driving while Brown), where people of color are routinely stopped for minor traffic violations. Philando Castile was pulled over because, according to the officer, he looked like someone who was involved in a robbery due to his wide-set nose, a trait common in Black people.[4] In this high-profile case that

Black men are pulled over by the police at higher rates than any other group due to racial profiling, a routine occurrence that comes with the risk of death.

mirrors many other recent fatal police shootings of Black people, Castile was pulled over for driving while Black, complied with the officer's request to show identification, and shot seconds after he calmly informed the officer that he had a legally permitted weapon on him.

Poor white people also benefit from better health outcomes than both poor and higher-income Black people. According to the Centers for Disease Control and Prevention, white men live more than four years longer than Black men, and white women live more than three years longer than Black women.[5] Black people are more likely to die from cancers that more white people survive, even though they experience cancer at the same rate.[6] Studies suggest that it is not socioeconomic status but racism that is the root of racial health disparities.[7] Prolonged exposure to racism causes chronic stress, which leads to poorer health outcomes for Native Americans and Black people at all socioeconomic levels.[8] Poor white people, despite any economic disadvantages, still have advantages that people of color cannot gain just by moving up the so-called economic ladder.

What About Black Privilege?

"We don't have a *White* History Month."

"If there was a group for *white* students at my school, that would be racist!"

"What about affirmative action? How is *that* fair?!"

The "what about us?" sentiment that leads to the idea that people of color are somehow privileged is a knee-jerk reaction to being faced with acknowledging that white privilege is in fact real. To understand that white privilege is real is to understand that people of color are largely oppressed, or disadvantaged by this country's institutions. Such systemic disadvantages require systemic solutions. As anti-racism educator and writer Tim Wise explained, this myth of Black privilege ignores the fact that the historical balance of power is always skewed in favor of whites, and viewing attempts to balance the scales as reverse discrimination ignores the social and historical context of race in our country. Wise says, "It's like protesting that sick people are privileged, relative to the healthy, because there are no hospitals for the latter. It's like complaining that the poor are privileged relative to the well-off because no one sets up soup kitchens to serve the affluent; nor does Habitat for Humanity ever show up to build mansions for the rich."[9]

The purpose of equality efforts is to ensure that all people in society have the same rights and access to opportunities and resources. Equality doesn't mean that everyone gets the same; that would imply that everyone starts life on equal footing. For white people in America, who are largely blind to the advantages they are so accustomed to, any efforts to create social equality might feel like oppression. No one really spends time thinking about the air that they breathe every day except the people who struggle to breathe for one reason or another. In that same way, white people are conditioned to be unaware of the rights and privileges that people of color struggle to gain access to. So when efforts such as affirmative action are put into place in higher education and the workplace, white people might perceive this as unfair. It in fact would be unfair if we ignored institutional racism, pretended that implicit bias doesn't exist, threw out everything we know about the history of race relations in America, and thought of whites and people of color as standing at the same starting line.

The History of Affirmative Action

In 1961, President John F. Kennedy signed Executive Order 10925, requiring government contractors to hire more women and minorities. Over the years, state and Supreme Court legislation expanded affirmative action, which was designed to level the playing field. Such affirmative action plans increased diversity in the workplace at faster rates than normal, according to one study. Studies also show there is no evidence that affirmative action forced employers to hire unqualified candidates—an idea that's largely rooted in biased ideas anyway.[10] Since the late 1990s, several states have reversed this legislation. In states that repealed affirmative action, compared to those that didn't, minority representation in state and local government jobs decreased significantly, with the decline continuing to grow for Black women.[11]

"But We Had a Black President!"

Barack Obama, elected president of the United States in 2008, was the first Black president in the country's history—more than two hundred years after the election of George Washington, the first president of the United States. In over two hundred years, Black people faced slavery, segregation, lynching, hate crimes, denial of rights, discrimination, and more. It would take a lot more than the election of a

President Barack Obama waves to the crowd after speaking at a summit.

single Black male president to prove that discrimination is no longer an issue in America. It's simply impossible for one two-term presidency to single-handedly dismantle the racist structures carved into the country's institutions and reverse centuries of white privilege.

In fact, Obama's presidency served as further proof that racism still exists and white privilege is real. During his campaign, opponents questioned his identity as American, claiming that he was born in Kenya and his birth certificate was forged. His Arabic middle name, Hussein, was used as a slur—an attempt to enforce the idea that he is an "other," not white, and therefore not to be trusted and unfit to run the country. The racist attempts to frame him as un-American followed him into his presidency. President Obama faced opposition from Congress at every turn. He was a perceived threat to white supremacy and a reminder that a country with such racist roots could never fully support a non-white, especially Black person, in such a position of power.

CHAPTER 5

Power and Responsibility

"With great power comes great responsibility." This well-known quote is attributed to the *Spider-Man* comics. However, when it comes to privilege and power, people of color don't need a superhero. People of color need white people to understand privilege and the role it plays in their lives and the lives of the oppressed. They need white people to understand the relationship between power and racism, and decide to take an active anti-racism approach in their everyday lives.

Understanding the Role of Power in Racism

When colonizers arrived in North America in 1492, an estimated five to fifteen million Indigenous people lived on the land. By the end of the nineteenth century, fewer than 238,000 remained.[1] Throughout the seventeeth century, settlers stole African people from

The Japanese were victims of extreme acts of racism. When Japanese Americans were forced into internment camps in the 1940s, they had committed no crime and an overwhelming majority of them were American citizens.

their land and tortured, killed, and enslaved them for free labor. In 1941, more than 100,000 Japanese Americans, most of whom were US citizens, were removed from their homes, schools, and lives and imprisoned in remote concentration camps for years.[2]

In 2002, President George W. Bush mandated a special registry targeting and surveilling visitors from Muslim-majority countries—a discriminatory practice that President Donald Trump attempted to reinstate in 2017.[3] These acts of racism were fueled by many things, including greed, hate, and fear. Though anyone can feel these feelings, power is what allowed white people to follow through on them. White people can begin to attempt to understand the experiences of people of color by recognizing that they have not in the history of America been persecuted for the color of their skin. They have been the majority, set the standards for what is normal and right, and everyone is fair game for judgment, discrimination, and racism by simply being non-white.

Black Lives Matter

Black Lives Matter is a movement that advocates for justice and fair treatment of Black people and is specifically a response to police violence against Blacks. All Lives Matter, the rebuttal to this movement, is an offensive display of white privilege. Not because all lives shouldn't matter, but because it is full of white privilege. Black lives continue to be threatened with every routine traffic stop and interaction with the police. By saying "All Lives Matter," White people, who do not have to fear for their lives during routine police interactions, are not only telling the oppressed how to fight for equality but are ignoring altogether that there even still is a fight.

Founders of the Black Lives Matter Movement Opal Tometi, Patrisse Cullors, and Alicia Garza

Understanding How Race Functions in Society

Another responsibility of those in power is to understand what affects those not in power and how. Because of the invisibility of white privilege, white people tend to take for granted how race affects people of color. Whether unawareness or conscious reluctance to recognize that both racism and white privilege are real, white people do a major disservice to race relations with these ideals. This disconnect between those in power and those with marginalized status must be addressed, but that requires that more white people interact with the reality of race.

People of color experience race daily. They are aware of their race and ethnicity when they turn on the television and the hardworking, loving families do not look like theirs. They are aware when they go to work and the grocery store. Not only are they constantly being reminded of their status as non-white in a society where white is the default, but they are more likely to socialize with a diverse circle of people. For some perspective, consider that about 70 percent of white people socialize with about 70 percent other white people.[4] About 60 percent also work with mostly other white people, while Hispanics and Blacks reported living in more diverse neighborhoods and having more diverse groups of friends.[5] This is more evidence that white people are allowed to go through life ignoring race. Survey results from CNN and the Kaiser Foundation show that people of color believe they experience discrimination in everyday situations. In the survey, 53 percent of Black people and 36 percent of

Hispanics reported experiencing racial discrimination in the last 30 days.[6] Interestingly, 15 percent of white people said they've dealt with such unfair treatment.[7] Though this small percentage reinforces the idea that white people are largely shielded from dealing with race on a daily basis, it also speaks to another phenomenon that displays a fundamental misunderstanding of how race operates in America.

Protesters outside of Baltimore City Hall on Thursday, April 30, 2015, following the death of Freddie Gray while in police custody

Defining Reverse Racism

Merriam-Webster defines racism as a belief that race is the primary determinant of human traits and capacities and that racial differences produce an inherent superiority of a particular race.[8] Dictionary.com defines racism as hatred or intolerance of another race or other races.[9] These definitions

seem to imply that anyone can experience racism and anyone can be racist. The problem with this is that dictionaries are made by people. Historically, the majority has the power and control over language and the meaning of words. So dictionary definitions themselves are chock-full of examples of white privilege in language. People of color, those actually affected by racism in America, have no say in how the word is defined. Writers and editors of dictionaries are largely white, and that has much influence over what language goes into dictionaries and what is considered unimportant.[10] Not only are dictionary definitions potentially biased, but when it comes to sociological terms, they simply lack the context and nuance necessary to aid understanding of such complex ideas. Hiding behind the dictionary definition of racism allows people in power to avoid checking their privilege.

Racism in America functions as a system, not individually. It is not a few police officers who need training or hate Black people. It is a country's entire police system that has been designed to control Black people—be it the eighteenth-century slave patrols whose

Mid-nineteenth-century engraving of a slave fleeing two slave hunters

main duties included chasing down runaway slaves, to the Jim Crow era where every aspect of daily life was racially segregated and so on—that is implicated in racism. Systems in this country were designed to keep whites in power. It is the power dynamic and privilege of whiteness that makes it impossible for reverse racism to exist.

Only oppressed people are subject to this institutionalized racism and lack the power to change it systematically. In America, whites have always held the most power, so the systems and institutions that exist today were all built this way and in order to keep it this way. The responsibility of those in power is to first recognize that race matters and attempt to understand the experiences of people of color instead of defaulting to the white-lens view of the world. Understanding white privilege and how it intersects with oppression and power to uphold white supremacy and doing nothing about it is to be complicit in systemic racism. White supremacy, the racial hierarchy in which whiteness reigns, is reinforced every time white people fail to acknowledge their white privilege and take active responsibility for how it affects people of color. Recognize that those who have the power to oppress also have the power to make change.

CHAPTER 6

Talking About Privilege

Recognizing and understanding white privilege is a great start, but it's not enough. In fact, acknowledging white privilege and doing nothing about it is problematic. Talking about it is the next best step because it begins to bring whiteness and its privileges into the everyday lexicon, which helps to close the racial disconnect. Remember, people of color are already aware of the ways in which white privilege negatively affects their lives. There will be strong feelings such as defensiveness, guilt, and fear to reckon with in these conversations. However, not being prepared or feeling scared or inadequate can no longer be an excuse not to engage in the conversations that will help move race relations forward. This white fragility derails conversations about race and stops the actions of fighting against white supremacy before they even start.

An Inner Dialogue About Privilege

A good place to start the conversation about white privilege is with yourself. Ask yourself:

- Have you ever been tasked with representing your entire race in conversation?

- Has your intelligence ever been questioned because of the color of your skin?

- Can you expect to see positive representations of people of your race every time you turn on the television or watch a movie?

- If necessary, can you call the police and rest assured that they will assist you and not harm you when they arrive?

- Can you go shopping without being followed around the store or being extra cautious that you don't look suspicious?

- When you succeed, do people assume it was on merit or because you were given a "hand?"

- Are your teachers, doctors, and other professionals and authority figures mostly the same race as you? Do you worry that any of these people are capable of racially discrimination discriminating against you?

- Can you go most places without the anxiety of being the only person of your skin color there and feeling alienated, odd, or unwelcome?

Reflect on the ways in which your race positions your social status and affects you on a daily basis. Asking yourself which of your experiences are a result of your race or ethnicity

People of color don't take for granted that everyday items, such as "flesh-colored" bandages, are constant reminders that white is the default.

is a practice in awareness. People of color are forced to do this every day. Seemingly minor things such as a trip to the store remind people of color that they are outsiders. Nude bandages are designed to be the color of white skin. Hair products for Black people are in an "ethnic hair care" section, positioned separately from the main hair care products. Celebrities on magazines mostly represent white standards of beauty and are prominently featured. White privilege serves its benefactors in thousands of ways each day, and increased awareness of those many ways helps bridge the disconnect in the conversation about privilege.

Talking with People of Color About White Privilege

When it comes to engaging people of color in discussion about white privilege or responding to people of color in general, awareness of white privilege is only one piece of the puzzle. Because talking about white privilege brings up feelings of guilt and defensiveness, white people need to be aware of the language being used in this discussion. This defensiveness can give white people the urge to prove they themselves are not racist. Out of that urge comes phrases such as "I don't see color," and "We're all the same." These phrases, no matter how well-intentioned, minimize the actual realities of race that people of color deal with. Colorblindness is a portrayal of white privilege. It allows white people, who benefit from their race, to ignore the discrimination that people of color face because of theirs.

Another tool to avoid in conversation with people of color is the dismissive "You're playing the race card." Writer Andrew Hernandez explains why the phrase is dangerous as part of the dialogue on race and white privilege: "It's more comfortable to gaslight people of color who mention race than it is to recognize how white people have benefited from and been complicit in reproducing racist structures."[1]

"You're playing the race card" is one of the most harmful tools in the invisible knapsack of white privilege. It presumes that white people know better than people of color, even in matters of racism. It dismisses the lived experiences of people of color—experiences that white people have not lived through the same lens. To avoid dismissing and diminishing experiences of people of color, white people should seek to analyze the situation and ask questions that attempt to understand the perspective of people of color as opposed to disprove it. For example, when Black people are grieving and expressing outrage over the most recent incident of fatal police brutality, resist the urge to deny it's about race to

"Playing the race card" is a phrase used as a weapon by white people who want to silence people of color instead of recognizing how they have benefited from racist systems.

justify the oppressive actions. Listen to Black people discuss the endless racial profiling that leads to these incidents in the first place. Ask if the victim were white, how would the interaction have gone differently. Ask yourself and people of color how differently the media might have covered the story. Think of examples that reinforce the point of view people of color are presenting instead of denying that race plays a part.

Taking Action

Race theory scholar and civil rights activist Derrick Bell once said that the battle against racism would not be won in court and legislation but in the consciousness of the people.[2] In order to work on the consciousness of the people, white people must talk to each other about white privilege. Here are some guidelines:

Ignore Feelings

Ignoring emotions goes against the most basic principle of how to deal with feelings. In the case of talking about white privilege, it's the first thing that white people need to leave at the door. White fragility is the stress response that white people have when talking about race. It triggers a fight-or-flight response. In conversation with people of color, it triggers anger, fear, and guilt. In the comfort of talking to other white people about race, it turns into justifying, denying, and endorsing each other's feelings and deflection. This desire for comfort is harmful to forward progression and is something that people of color do not get the luxury of.

Stop Focusing on the Positive

This, again, seems like a counterintuitive approach to dealing with a problem. However, would it be appropriate to go to a funeral and tell the grieving to cheer up and look on the bright side? Throwing around words and phrases about love and forgiveness and talking about how things could be worse are not only a deflection but are damaging and insulting to people of color. These words do nothing to move the conversation forward. Instead of focusing on the positive, focus squarely on the negative and examine how your position as a white person can or has contributed to the problem

Conversations between white people and people of color about race can easily turn into heated arguments when white people respond defensively. It is not, however, the duty of people of color to manage the feelings of a white person in conversations that already require a lot of emotional labor from people who experience their race and racism every day.

and and can contribute to the solution. White people who tell each other that they are indeed "good people" will undoubtedly feel good about themselves, but they will have done nothing to broaden their perspectives.

Use Your Privilege

The ultimate goal in looking at privilege and power is to do something with it—specifically anti-racism actions. Being anti-racist is an action. It is not a passive way of being. It is hard work, and white people should not expect to get a certificate of appreciation from people of color for doing this necessary work. People of color have

been doing free or cheap labor in this country for centuries, and managing the feelings of white people is not another free labor they should take on.

Being a true ally in the fight against racism requires an understanding and acknowledgment of white privilege but most importantly a good look at the struggle and fight of those negatively impacted by it.

As people of color fight for equality, white people have the weapon of white privilege that they can choose to bring to the fight. White people can use that weapon to help dismantle racist systems. Stop other white people mid-sentence when they use racially coded language, such as "ghetto," "thug," and "Black-on-Black crime." Use the opportunity to share what you know about racial profiling and segregated communities. Ask white authority figures why it appears that your peers of color are getting harsher punishments than your white peers. Seek out and demand that your school include books from authors of color in the curriculum. People of color do not need white saviors. Using white privilege should be seen as a duty rather than a grand experience meant to validate that privilege. White people must embrace the discomfort that comes with recognizing white privilege and resolve to actively use that privilege for the good of those with less power in this society.

Chapter Notes

Introduction

1. Saba Hamedy, "The Parkland kids keep checking their privilege," CNN.com, March 25, 2018, https://www.cnn.com/2018/03/24/politics/march-for-our-lives-students-checking-privilege-trnd/index.html.
2. Dakin Andoneh, CNN.com, March 24, 2018, https://www.cnn.com/2018/03/24/us/naomi-wadler-march-for-our-lives-black-girls-trnd/index.html.

Chapter 1
Privilege and Power Explained

1. W. E. B. Du Bois, *Black Reconstruction in America: An Essay Toward a History of the Part Which Black Folk Played in the Attempt to Reconstruct Democracy in America*, 1860–1880 (New York: The Free Press, 1965), p. 700.
2. Ibid.
3. Ibid.
4. "African American Life During the Great Depression and the New Deal," Britannica.com, accessed March 2018, https://www.britannica.com/topic/African-American/African-American-life-during-the-Great-Depression-and-the-New-Deal.
5. "Black Codes," History.com, accessed March 2018, http://www.history.com/topics/black-history/black-codes.
6. Jim Wallis, *America's Original Sin: Racism, White Privilege, and the Bridge to a New America*. Grand Rapids, MI: Brazos, a Division of Baker Group, 2017.

Chapter 2
Examining White Privilege

1. Samantha Neal, "Views of racism as a major problem increase sharply, especially among Democrats," PewResearch.org, August 29, 2017, http://www.pewresearch.org/fact-tank/2017/08/29/

views-of-racism-as-a-major-problem-increase-sharply-especially-among-democrats.

2. McIntosh, Peggy. (2000). *White Privilege: Unpacking the Invisible Knapsack*. Louisville Anarchist Federation and No Borders, 30.

3. Reed Jordan, "High-poverty schools undermine education for children of color," Urban.org, May 20, 2015, https://www.urban.org/urban-wire/high-poverty-schools-undermine-education-children-color.

4. Ibid.

5. Ibid.

6. Lindsey Cook, "U.S. Education: Still Separate and Unequal," *US News and World Report*, January 28, 2015, https://www.usnews.com/news/blogs/data-mine/2015/01/28/us-education-still-separate-and-unequal.

7. Gillian B. White, "Public School Funding and the Role of Race," *Atlantic*, September 30, 2015, https://www.theatlantic.com/business/archive/2015/09/public-school-funding-and-the-role-of-race/408085.

8. Associated Press, "Linda Brown, student in 1954 ruling ending school segregation, dies," NBCNews.com, March 26, 2018, https://www.nbcnews.com/news/us-news/linda-brown-student-1954-ruling-ending-school-segregation-dies-n860226.

9. "Race," US Census Bureau, accessed March 2018, https://www.census.gov/topics/population/race/about.html.

10. David Andolfatto, "Why Do Unemployment Rates Vary by Race and Ethnicity?" Federal Reserve Bank of St. Louis, February 6, 2017, https://www.stlouisfed.org/on-the-economy/2017/february/why-unemployment-rates-vary-races-ethnicity.

11. Ibid.

12. "The Mystery of High Unemployment Rates for Black Americans," *Economist*, August 3, 2017, https://www.economist.com/blogs/graphicdetail/2017/08/daily-chart-1.

13. "Racial, gender wage gaps persist in U.S. despite some progress," Pew Research Center, July 1, 2016, http://www.pewresearch.org/fact-tank/2016/07/01/racial-gender-wage-gaps-persist-in-u-s-despite-some-progress.
14. Ibid.
15. "Wealth, Asset Ownership, & Debt of Households Detailed Tables: 2013," Census.gov, May 4, 2017, https://www.census.gov/data/tables/2013/demo/wealth/wealth-asset-ownership.html.
16. Sara Boboltz and Kimberly Yam, "Why On-Screen Representation Actually Matters," *Huffington Post*, February 24, 2017, https://www.huffingtonpost.com/entry/why-on-screen-representation-matters_us_58aeae96e4b01406012fe49d.
17. Travis L. Dixon, "A Dangerous Distortion of Our Families," ColorOfChange.org, December 2017, https://colorofchange.org/dangerousdistortion.
18. Jeremy Borden and Todd C. Frankel, "Dylann Roof's teenage years marked by father's bitter divorce," WashingtonPost.com, June 22, 2015, https://www.washingtonpost.com/news/post-nation/wp/2015/06/22/dylann-roofs-teenage-years-marked-by-fathers-bitter-divorce.
19. Ibid.

Chapter 3
Intersections of Privilege and Oppression

1. "Oppression," Marilyn Frye, http://www.filosoficas.unam.mx/docs/327/files/Marilyn%20Frye,%20Oppression.pdf.
2. Ashley Crossman, "Definition of Social Oppression," ThoughtCo.com, March 6, 2017, https://www.thoughtco.com/social-oppression-3026593.
3. "Women's Suffrage," History.com, accessed April 2018, https://www.history.com/topics/womens-history/the-fight-for-womens-suffrage.

4. "The State of the Gender Pay Gap 2018," Payscale.com, accessed April 2018, https://www.payscale.com/data-packages/gender-pay-gap.

5. Ibid.

6. "Sexual Violence," Centers for Disease Control and Prevention, accessed March 2018, https://www.cdc.gov/features/sexualviolence/index.html.

7. Lianna Brinded, "The unexpected, paradigm-shifting power of #MeToo," October 7, 2017, https://qz.com/1104276/metoo.

8. Drew Desilver, "5 Facts About the Minimum Wage," Pew Research Center, January 4, 2017, http://www.pewresearch.org/fact-tank/2017/01/04/5-facts-about-the-minimum-wage.

9. Emmie Martin, "Here's how much housing prices have skyrocketed over the last 50 years," CNBC.com, June 23, 2017, https://www.cnbc.com/2017/06/23/how-much-housing-prices-have-risen-since-1940.html.

10. Christianna Silva, "LGBT Youth are More than 120% Likely to Be Homeless," Newsweek.com, November 30, 2017, http://www.newsweek.com/lgbt-youth-homeless-study-727595.

11. "nTIDE December 2017 Jobs Report: Year-end Job Numbers Cap Record Year for Americans with Disabilities," Research on Disability, January 5, 2018, https://researchondisability.org/news-features/2018/01/05/ntide-december-2017-jobs-report-year-end-job-numbers-cap-record-year-for-americans-with-disabilities.

12. "Disability Barriers," CDC.gov, accessed March 2018, https://www.cdc.gov/ncbddd/disabilityandhealth/disability-barriers.html.

13. Christianna Silva, "LGBT Youth are More than 120% Likely to Be Homeless," Newsweek.com, November 30, 2017, http://www.newsweek.com/lgbt-youth-homeless-study-727595.

14. Ibid.

Chapter 4
The Myths of Privilege

1. Emily Badger, "Black Poverty Differs from White Poverty," *Washington Post*, August 12, 2015, http://www.washingtonpost.com/news/wonk/wp/2015/08/12/black-poverty-differs-from-white-poverty.
2. "Cities with high racial economic inequality and widespread poverty increase police force size," Phys.org, August 8, 2013, https://phys.org/news/2013-08-cities-high-racial-economic-inequality.html.
3. Ibid.
4. Jon Schuppe, "Officer Mistook Philando Castile for a Robbery Suspect, Tapes Show," NBCnews.com, July 21, 2016, https://www.nbcnews.com/news/us-news/officer-thought-philando-castile-was-robbery-suspect-tapes-show-n607856.
5. Elizabeth Arias, "Changes in Life Expectancy by Race and Hispanic Origin in the United States, 2013–2014," CDC.gov, April 2016, https://www.cdc.gov/nchs/products/databriefs/db244.htm.
6. "Cancer Facts & Figures for African Americans," Cancer.org, accessed March 2018, https://www.cancer.org/research/cancer-facts-statistics/cancer-facts-figures-for-african-americans.html.
7. Jason Silverstein, "Genes Don't Cause Racial-Health Disparities, Society Does," *Atlantic*, April 13, 2015, https://www.theatlantic.com/health/archive/2015/04/genes-dont-cause-racial-health-disparities-society-does/389637.
8. Rochaun Meadows-Fernandez, "Even as Black Americans Get Richer, Their Health Outcomes Remain Poor," *Pacific Standard Magazine*, January 23, 2018, https://psmag.com/social-justice/even-as-black-americans-get-richer-their-health-outcomes-remain-poor.
9. Russell Huebsch, "Affirmative Action & Ethnic Diversity in the Workplace," SmallBusiness.chron.com, accessed April 2018, http://smallbusiness.chron.com/affirmative-action-ethnic-diversity-workplace-4929.html.
10. Fidan Ana Kurtulus, "The Impact of Eliminating Affirmative Action on Minority and Female Employment: A Natural Experiment

Approach Using State-Level Affirmative Action Laws and EEO-4 Data," Harvard.edu, October 2013, http://gap.hks.harvard.edu/impact-eliminating-affirmative-action-minority-and-female-employment-natural-experiment-approach.

11. Ibid.

Chapter 5
Power and Responsibility

1. Donald L. Fixico, "When Native Americans Were Slaughtered in the Name of 'Civilization,'" History.com, March 2, 2018, https://www.history.com/news/native-americans-genocide-united-states.

2. "Civil Rights: Japanese Americans," PBS.org, accessed April 2018, http://www.pbs.org/thewar/at_home_civil_rights_japanese_american.htm.

3. Kaveh Waddell, "America Already Had a Muslim Registry," *Atlantic*, December 20, 2016, https://www.theatlantic.com/technology/archive/2016/12/america-already-had-a-muslim-registry/511214.

4. Jennifer Agiesta, "Race and Reality in America: Five Key Findings," CNN.com, November 25,2015, https://www.cnn.com/2015/11/24/us/race-reality-key-findings/index.html.

5. Ibid.

6. Ibid.

7. Ibid.

8. "Racism," Merriam-Webster.com, accessed April 2018, https://www.merriam-webster.com/dictionary/racism.

9. "Racism," Dictionary.com, accessed April 2018, http://www.dictionary.com/browse/racism.

10. "Why Using the Dictionary Definition of Racism Just Doesn't Work," EverdayFeminism.com, March 15, 2015, https://everydayfeminism.com/2015/03/dictionary-definition-racism.

Chapter 6

Talking About Privilege

1. Andrew Hernández, "Let's Expose the White Double Standard for 'Playing the Race Card'," *Establishment*, May 13, 2017, https://theestablishment.co/lets-expose-the-white-double-standard-for-playing-the-race-card-4dfee1738f84.
2. Kenneth B. Nunn, "The R-Word: A Tribute to Derrick Bell," Scholarship. law.ufl.edu, 2011, https://scholarship.law.ufl.edu/cgi/viewcontent.cgi?article=1367.

Glossary

anti-racism Actions and practices that oppose racism and promote racial equality.

bias Prejudice in favor of or against a group of people; includes implicit bias, which is unconscious prejudiced beliefs and attitudes.

centering Focusing on the white perspective or experience by using white as the default and the starting point.

criminalization Turning a person or groups of people into criminals by making activities associated with those groups of people illegal.

institutions Includes the courts, government, church, organizations, corporations, schools, the media, banks, healthcare, and the criminal justice system.

intersectionality Coined by Black legal scholar Kimberlé Crenshaw, a term referring to the way the effects of different forms of discrimination, such as racism, sexism, and classism, overlap and intersect.

marginalized The status of groups of people who are given lower status in society by way of stripping them of an active voice, identity, or place in it.

oppression Prolonged cruel and unjust treatment meant to keep people from gaining power and status.

racially coded Language that appears to mean one thing on the surface but has a negative connotation targeted at racial and ethnic minorities.

representation The media portrayal of people as being a certain way, which helps shape ideas about groups of people.

systemic racism Prejudice and discrimination that is embedded in the social institutions in our country.

white fragility The emotional stress response of white people to discussions about race.

white savior A narrative where white people rescue people of color.

whiteness The ways in which being white function in society and give privilege to white people.

Further Reading

Books

Birchett, Colleen, et al. *The New Jim Crow: Mass Incarceration in the Age of Colorblindness*. Chicago, IL: Samuel DeWitt Proctor Conference, Inc., 2011.

Coates, Ta-Nehisi, and Klaus Amann. *Between the World and Me*. Ditzingen, Germany: Reclam, 2017.

Rothenberg, Paula S. *White Privilege: Essential Readings on the Other Side of Racism*. New York, NY: Worth Publishers, 2015.

Wise, Tim J. *White Like Me: Reflections on Race from a Privileged Son*. New York, NY: Soft Skull Press, 2011.

Websites

Black Lives Matter
www.blacklivesmatter.com
The official site of the Black Lives Matter movement, which offers opportunities to engage in activism and information about coordinating racial equality events.

Showing Up for Racial Justice
www.showingupforracialjustice.org
A movement lead by people of color to organize white people for social change.

Teaching Tolerance
www.tolerance.org
Educational resources that emphasize social justice and anti-bias to help people challenge prejudice.

Index